SCANSION OF THE

Michèle Finck is a poet, critic, translator, librettist, screen-writer, and professor at the University of Strasbourg. She received the Prix Louise-Labé (2015) and the Prix Max-Jacob (2018) for her poetry. She often collaborates with artists (painters, musicians, cineasts, choreographers). She has published essays on contemporary poetry (Yves Bonnefoy) and on the dialogue between poetry and other arts. A special number of the electronic magazine *Nu(e)* was devoted to her work in 2019 (number 69, 400 pages), edited by Patrick Née.

Since 1969 **Anthony Rudolf** has published poetry and prose, the latter including fiction, memoirs, art and literary criticism, politics and war studies. He has translated books, mainly poetry, from the French, Russian and other languages. He has also translated art books. His literary essays include texts on authors as diverse as Balzac, Byron, Borges, George Oppen and Primo Levi, and on poetry written in extreme situations. He has written widely on visual artists, including Paula Rego, R.B.Kitaj and Charlotte Salomon.

Also by Michèle Finck

La Ballade des hommes-nuages   (éditions Arfuyen, 2022)

Sur un piano de paille, Variations Goldberg avec cri (éditions Arfuyen, 2020)

Connaissance par les larmes   (éditions Arfuyen, 2017)

La troisième main   (éditions Arfuyen, 2015)

Balbuciendo   (éditions Arfuyen, 2012)

Also by Anthony Rudolf

Pedraterra   (Odd Volumes, 2021)

The Binding of Isaac [Rosenberg]   (Shoestring Press, 2021)

Journey Around my Flat   (Shearsman, 2021)

European Hours: Collected Poems   (Carcanet, 2017)

Jerzyk's Diary   (Shearsman, 2016)

Silent Conversations   (Seagull Books, 2013)

Scansion of the Dark

Michèle Finck
Translated by Anthony Rudolf

Broken Sleep Books

ISBN: 978-1-915760-45-6

Cover designed by Aaron Kent

Edited and Typeset by Aaron Kent

Broken Sleep Books Ltd
Rhydwen
Talgarreg
Ceredigion
SA44 4HB

Broken Sleep Books Ltd
Fair View
St Georges Road
Cornwall
PL26 7YH

Contents

Je suis devenue chant et destin
— Anna Akhmatova

I have became song and destiny
— Anna Akhmatova

Preface
— Michèle Finck

Scansion of the Dark is a complete sequence drawn from a longer book: **Balbuciendo*. This dark work, dense and harsh, gravitates around the experience of loss and farewell. *Balbuciendo* is composed in three movements: *On the Blade of Farewell* (loss of the lover), *Triptych for the Dead Father*, and *Scansion of the Dark*, which is an alchemical attempt at transmuting loss into a scansion of shadows, into poetry. The years during which *Scansion of the Dark* was written were years of turning-in on the self and of monastic poetical work, indissociable from a meditation on everyday life, focussing on the fundamental question posed by Rilke in his *Letters to a Young Poet*: "Would you die if you were forbidden to write?"

Scansion of the Dark is composed of fifteen poems, each of which can be read simultaneously as an epitaph of the tomb-book *Balbuciendo* and as a paradoxical lesson of life. This tomb could have culminated in complete silence, which is always present in the foundations of language. But, in *Scansion of the Dark*, the poetic voice is extracted live from this tomb and comprehends that one can bear the dark if one scans it, if one gives it a rhythm, if one converts loss into the energy of writing. In suffering, the poetic voice learns to become *song* and *fate*, in the words of Anna Akhmatova borrowed for the epigraph to *Scansion of the Dark*. It remains essential, for this difficult conversion to be achieved, to undergo the ordeals of personal and transpersonal memory, solitude faced with the void, sickness, crying out, physical and psychic distress, all of which assail poetic consciousness. Existence and verses are reduced to their hard kernel designated by the key vocable, "bone". Faced with separation and death, one stammers, and therefore poetry, if it wishes to speak the truth about life, can only be written *balbuciendo*: "Poem: scansion of the dark, *balbuciendo*."

But out of the violence done to body and language (images, sounds, rhythms in permanent crisis), a strength is finally born which battles against suffering, revives words, brings back to life the material of sonority, regenerates the reader. *Balbuciendo* can also be read as musical notation on a score, and here the music does not cease haunting the words. The poem, condition of life, one's only travelling companion in the dark, does not bring salvation but succeeds in being a "scanner" which reveals the depths of the human condition in a living form. "Let the poem / Scan the dark/ Torn from the ear". After the orphic descent incarnated by the first two movements of *Balbuciendo*, the third movement of the book. *Scansion of the Dark*, where suffering is encountered and surmounted, signals a movement of escape from hell, rising with a song that is mournful but more beautiful, even universal, because it has known hell. To the question "what does poetry owe to hell?", *Scansion of the Dark*, a fate-work, replies: its lucidity, its hand-to-hand battle with language, its strength, its scansion which awakens what is possible and permits one to believe in it again.

*Translator's note:
the Spanish word for "stammering" is untranslated in the original.

Scriptorium

Écriture : tour, terre, terrier, trou.

À-pic du cri dans l'œil de la gorge.

Les mots titubent atterrés de mémoire.

Les souvenirs brûlent le vagin du visage.

Une étoile anonyme essuie les larmes.

Les onomatopées de l'os tournoient.

Poème : scansion du noir, *balbuciendo*.

Scriptorium

Writing: tower, earth, burrow, hole.
Cry's cliff in the eye of the throat.
Words totter overwhelmed by souvenance.
Memories scorch the vagina of the face.
A star, anonymous, wipes away the tears.
Onomatopoeias of the bone turn round.
Poem: scansion of the dark, *balbuciendo*.

Même décapité
Le tournesol éclaire
La bouche sans langue.

Even decapitated
The sunflower lights up
The tongueless mouth

Musique interdite

J'ai longtemps hiberné dans mon oreille.
Mais vint un soir de cri où je n'ai plus cru
À la musique. Des transes me tordaient
D'orgasmes sonores morts.
Dard dans la nuit du crâne.
Seules les larmes balbutiaient de soleils et d'étoiles.

J'ai osé désosser la musique. Elle a laissé
Une large cicatrice ventriloque sur ma carcasse
Couturée. Maintenant mes pieds sont cloués
Aux mues des mots. Comment marcher si la musique
Ne me précède plus ? Et si l'âme du violon
Crame de trop d'excréments de mémoire ?

Forbidden Music

I have hibernated a long time in my ear.
But one evening came a cry and I no longer
Believed in music. Trances twisted me
Into sonorous dead orgasms.
Darts in the darkness of my skull.
Only tears stammered out suns and stars.

I have dared to bone up on music,
Leaving a large ventriloquial scar
On my carcass. Now my feet are nailed
To the moults of words. How can I walk
If music no longer leads the way?
And if the soul of the violin
Burns from too much excrement of memory?

Soif

Croquis d'agonie sur les draps crevassés
Par l'insomnie. Feu dans les meurtrières du crâne.
Visage vissé au mur de la douleur.
L'empreinte digitale de ton âme
Est posée à jamais sur mes paupières.
Je chancèle de trop de mémoire.

Les pieds nus font l'aumône.
Les souvenirs tremblent à la commissure du vagin.
Le soleil se couche toujours seul.
Il vomit des bouches mortes.
Le doux ventre blanc de la pie apaise.
Le corps s'éboule. J'ai mangé ma mémoire.

Poème : don qui porte secours.
Mais laisse la soif et la brûlure.

Thirst

Sketches of death-struggle on sheets cracked
By insomnia. Fire in the skull's murderesses.
Face screwed to the wall of sorrow.
The fingerprint of your soul
Rests forever on my eyelids.
I stagger from an overdose of souvenance.

Bare feet give alms.
Memories tremble at the vagina's commissure.
The sun sets always alone.
It vomits dead mouths.
The sweet white belly of the magpie assuages.
The body crumbles. I have eaten my souvenance.

Poem: gift which offers assistance.
But leaves behind thirst and burning.

Soliloque

Je m'appelle Seule. J'ai brûlé
Dans l'abcès d'une langue
Étrangère. Muette.
Maintenant sèves d'oreilles
Savent. Orages de sons
Crèvent dans la tête. Trou
Béant au fond de l'alphabet.

Je m'appelle Seule. Arborescence
De mots anonymes au bout des doigts.
Ai-je cru neiger entre les bras d'un fou
Sublime ? Maintenant je peins
Les cicatrices de l'invisible en noir.
Ce peu de buée de sons qui tremble
Sur la page déchirée me suffit.

Soliloquy

My name is Solitude. I have burned
In the abscess of a foreign
Tongue. Dumb.
Now auricular sap
Knows. Sound storms
Burst in my head. Gaping
Hole in the deep of the alphabet.

My name is Solitude. Arborescence
Of anonymous words at the tips of my fingers.
Did I believe I was snowing in the arms of a sublime
Fool? Now I paint
The scars of the invisible in black.
This little haze of sounds trembling
On the torn page suffices me.

Poème : peau d'âme
Morceau de lave arraché
Au cri de quel Vésuve ?

Poem: soul skin

Fragment of lava torn

From the cry of what Vesuvius?

L'os atroce

Le cerisier se couvre de fleurs et moi je perds
Les miennes. Toutes. Sauf une. Blanche.
Obstinée. Inarrachée jusque-là. Aile unique
Aiguë plantée dans le sacrum. Quand elle tombera
Je tomberai avec elle. Suicide sans traces. Qui
Nous ramassera ? Cette fleur, celle qui résiste,
Personne ne l'a jamais comprise. Pas toi. Moi non plus.
C'est elle qui fleurit en mots et fleurira jusqu'au bout.
Malgré elle. Pour rien. Bonne qu'à ça.
Le forsythia est en fleurs cette nuit
Sur le masque mortuaire de la douceur.

Unbearable Bone

The cherry tree is covered with blossoms and I have lost
All mine. Except one. White.
Stubborn. Untorn off as yet. Unique sharp
Wing planted in the sacrum. When it falls
I shall fall with it. Suicide without trace. Who
Shall pick us up? This blossom, which resists,
No one has ever understood it. Not you. Not me.
It's the one which flowers in words and will flower until the end.
Despite it. For nothing. All it's good for.
The forsythia is in bloom tonight
Over the death mask of tenderness.

À un revenant

Rumeur de mimosa dans la mémoire.

Que murmure-t-elle à l'espoir qui écoute

Les étoiles filantes se fracasser dans l'œil ?

Traces de pas sur la neige rouge de la mémoire.

De qui sont ces pas ? Taches de cris. De qui ces cris ?

Illisible mémoire déchiffrée comme en rêve

Les yeux bandés. Qui te hante ? Quel revenant

Au visage masqué et balafré de larmes qui ordonne :

Soit le poème

        scanner de l'obscur

                arraché à l'ouïe ?

To a Ghost

Rumour of mimosa in memory.
What does memory murmur to the hope
That listens to the falling stars
As they crash to pieces in the eye?
Traces of steps in the red snow of memory.
Whose steps are these? Stains of cries. Whose these cries?
Illegible memory deciphered as in dream
Eyes blindfolded. Who haunts you? What ghost
Masked and scarred with tears, who gives the order:
Shall the poem

        scan the dark

                torn out of the ear?

Convalescence

Se hisser hors de la chambre sépulcrale
Et du cercueil du cerveau. Apercevoir
Les branches du cerisier : grands cygnes en vol
Aux ailes rayonnantes de fleurs.
Se courber au-dessus de la chrysalide
Des non-nés et du cantique de leurs crânes.

« Qu'as-tu fait, crient-ils, qu'as-tu fait
De ta chevelure de lilas blancs et de ta robe
Transparente en rumeurs de fleurs de cerisier ?

-L'alchimiste caboche les a calcinées.
La fournaise de la mémoire les a noircies.
Je neige de pétales foudroyés.
La neige est bègue. La bouche bâillonnée
Haillonnée de mots sans repos. »

Convalescence

Hoist oneself out of the sepulchral bedroom
And the coffin of the brain. Observe
The branches of the cherry tree: great swans in flight,
Their wings radiant with blossoms.
Bend over the chrysalis
Of the unborn and the canticle of their skulls.

"What have you done, they cry, what have you done
To your white-lilac hair and your dress
Transparent in rumours of cherry trees?

— The alchemical bonce has burnt them to a cinder.
The furnace of memory has blackened them.
I snow blasted petals.
The snow is stuttering. The gagged mouth
Is tattered with restless words".

Poème :

Fil de funambule tendu entre pierre tombale

Et perce-neige.

Poem:

Tightrope walker's cord

Stretched between tombstone and snowdrop.

Bégaiement

Cratère de fatigue, ventrale, cervicale. Assez.

La lumière d'hiver crie d'anges que je ne peux rejoindre.

La douleur tord la chevelure d'hortensia de la mémoire.

Une voix de ruminant bégaie à l'oreille :

« Dieu me meut ». Ou est-ce : « Dieu me

Ment » ? Le destin se joue à la lettre près

Et on n'entend pas distinctement cette lettre.

Mais le tapage cesse. Un peu de bleu monte au crâne.

Chaque côte est peinte en or par un peintre invisible :

Échelle intérieure à gravir jusqu'à l'œil du cœur.

Stuttering

Crater of fatigue. Ventral. Cervical. Enough.
The light of winter cries angels I cannot join.
Grief twists the hortensia hair of memory.
A ruminant's voice stutters in the ear:
God moves me. Or does God lie to me?
Destiny is played out to the letter.
One does not hear this letter clearly.
But the uproar ceases. A touch of blue rises in the skull.
Each rib is painted in gold by an invisible painter:
Interior ladder to climb up to the heart's core.

À l'écoute

Chute de grêle dans la tête. Ronde de ronces.
Je ronge les os d'un ancien amour. Asthme`
De la mémoire. Spasme du passé. Le couteau
Du cri s'agenouille dans le ventre et prie. Et pas
Un moignon de silence pour peindre le noir des nuits.

À quel moment le mot ment ? L'écoute le sait
Qui ouvre le crâne des sons et caresse de ses mains
Anonymes les mots béants et bègues. Sa peau
D'eau de source apaise le souffle et laisse

Des noms neiger hors du nombril du noir.

To Listening

Hail falling in the head. Round of thorns.
I gnaw the bones of a former love. Asthma
Of memory. Spasms of the past. The knife
Of the cry kneels in the belly and prays. And no
Stump of silence to paint the darkness of the nights.

At what moment does the word lie? Listening knows
Which opens up the skull of sounds, and caresses
With its anonymous hands the gaping stuttering words.
Its skin of spring water calms the breath and lets

Names snow out of the navel of darkness

Line 6. Untranslatable pun in the original: "A quel moment le mot ment?"

À la couleur

J'ai cru griffer le ciel jusqu'au sang
Mais le ciel ne saigne pas.

Quand le prince de la couleur viendra-t-il
Enluminer nos corps de sa salive multicolore ?
Quand peindra-t-il en nous ses fresques silencieuses ?
Seul vient un mendiant de mots, chargé de nuit.
Nous nous agenouillons tous deux au bord de l'os,
Inconsolables, pour pleurer l'implosion de la couleur.

Le noir est la seule vérité de la bouche.

Ce soir un peu de bleu a eu pitié de moi
Et s'est posé sur mon front comme une étoile.

To Colour

I thought I scratched the sky till it bled
But the sky does not bleed.

When will the prince of colour come
And illuminate our bodies with his many-coloured saliva?
When will he paint his silent frescoes upon us?
Alone arrives a beggar of words, laden with night.
We both kneel on the edge of the bone,
Inconsolable, weeping the implosion of colour.

The dark is the only truth of the mouth.

This evening a spot of blue took pity on me
And rose up on my forehead like a star.

Tremblement
Sur le piano noir
D'un flocon de neige.

Trembling
Upon the black piano
Of a snowflake

Ciel silence cigale

J'écris

D'un seul coup tout autour des tortues sauvages.

Sky silence cicada
I write
At one fell swoop wild turtles all around

Acknowledgements

My thanks to Anthony Rudolf for his profound understanding of the poems and for the power of his translations. And many thanks to Broken Sleep Books.

— Michèle Finck

***

My thanks to Michèle Finck for her patient and insightful comments on early drafts of the translations and for writing a preface for this book. Thanks to Broken Sleep Books for taking the book on.

— Anthony Rudolf

EXPOSE TON MALAISE

Ingram Content Group UK Ltd.
Milton Keynes UK
UKHW040658060723
424652UK00006B/125